CREATE YOUR OWN COMICS

WORDS BY
NED HARTLEY

ART BY
ALEX LOPEZ

EDITED BY GARY PANTON
DESIGNED BY ZOE BRADLEY

Manufacturer: First published in Great Britain in 2026 by Buster Books, an imprint of
Michael O'Mara Books Limited, 9 Lion Yard, Tremadoc Road, London SW4 7NQ
www.mombooks.com

Represented by: Authorised Rep Compliance Ltd, Ground Floor,
71 Lower Baggot Street, Dublin D02 P593, Ireland
www.arccompliance.com

W www.mombooks.com/buster

f Buster Books

@buster_books

A CIP catalogue record for this book is available from the British Library.

ISBN: 978-1-91676-308-1

10 9 8 7 6 5 4 3 2 1

This book was printed in October 2025 by
Shenzhen Wing King Tong Paper Products Co. Ltd.,
Shenzhen, Guangdong, China.

For further information see www.mombooks.com/about/sustainability-climate-focus
Report any safety issues to product.safety@mombooks.com

CREATE YOUR OWN
COMICS

BUSTER BOOKS

CONTENTS

CHAPTER 3: TELLING YOUR STORY 47

CHAPTER 4: YOUR COMICS 73

INTRODUCTION

WHAT'S ONE THING THAT'S EVEN BETTER THAN READING COMICS? MAKING COMICS OF YOUR OWN!

THIS BOOK WILL TAKE YOU THROUGH EVERYTHING YOU NEED TO BECOME A COMIC MASTER. IT'S PACKED WITH HINTS, TIPS AND PROMPTS FOR COMING UP WITH STORIES, DEVELOPING YOUR OWN CHARACTERS AND SETTING YOUR IMAGINATION FREE. AT THE BACK OF THE BOOK, YOU'LL FIND EXTRA SPACE FOR SCRIBBLING DOWN YOUR IDEAS, AND A GLOSSARY TO HELP YOU UNDERSTAND SOME OF THE MOST COMMON COMIC TERMS.

WHEN YOU SEE BLANK SPACES, THEY'RE THERE FOR A REASON: FOR YOU TO FILL IN. THIS BOOK HAS BEEN CREATED FOR YOU TO PRACTISE WITH AND MAKE YOUR OWN, SO DON'T WORRY ABOUT MESSING IT UP. JUST GO FOR IT. GRAB YOUR PENS AND PENCILS, AND GO WILD!

Hi, I'm Com-X! I'm a robot who is programmed to love comics. I'm here to help you make your own brilliant comic stories.

CHAPTER 1
WHAT ARE COMICS?

HOW COMICS WORK

COMICS CAN LOOK CONFUSING TO A BEGINNER, BUT THEY'RE ACTUALLY REALLY SIMPLE TO UNDERSTAND. HERE ARE SOME BASICS OF HOW THEY WORK ...

You read comics from left to right. Start with the speech balloons at the top of the panel ...

... then read the ones below.

The pointy tail of the speech balloon tells you who is talking.

These comics are all mine. I TOLD you I love comics!

When you reach the end of a row of panels ...

... GO DOWN TO THE NEXT ROW!

Comics come in lots of different art styles ...

... but as long as you can draw a stick figure, you can make a comic!

What will your comic be about?

Lots of the best-known comics are about superheroes, but they don't have to be.

Comics can be about anything – or anyone – you like!

Unlike books with just words in them, comics use pictures to give the reader much of the info they need. I don't have to tell you we're suddenly in a classroom, because you can see for yourself!

Do you know what the difference is between a comic and a graphic novel?

Um ...

I can answer this one!

Comics are usually shorter, and can be just a few panels or pages long. Graphic novels are often longer, and can be entire books!

COMIC CREATOR
CHECKLIST

YOU DON'T NEED LOADS OF FANCY EQUIPMENT TO MAKE A COMIC, BUT HAVING THESE THINGS WILL HELP ...

DO YOU HAVE ...

A PENCIL? ☐

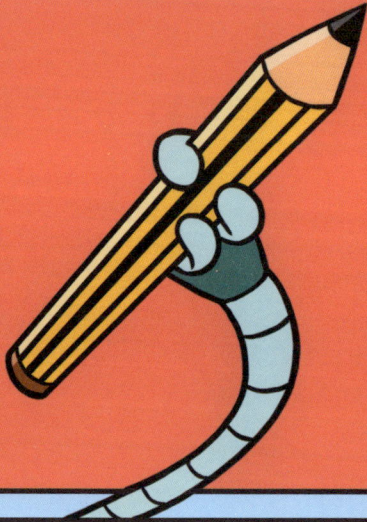

AN ERASER? ☐

AN INK PEN? ☐

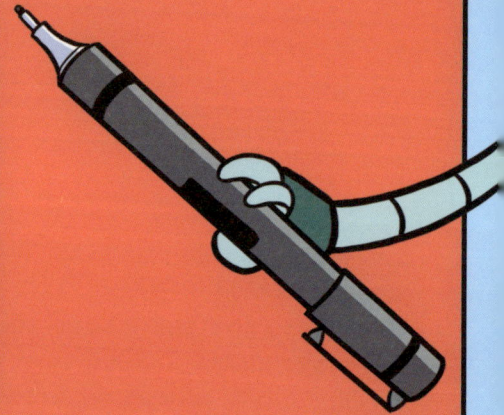

COLOURING PENS OR PENCILS? ☐

SNACKS TO KEEP YOU GOING? ☐

THE BEST IDEA FOR A COMIC THAT ANYONE HAS EVER HAD IN THE HISTORY OF THE UNIVERSE? ☐

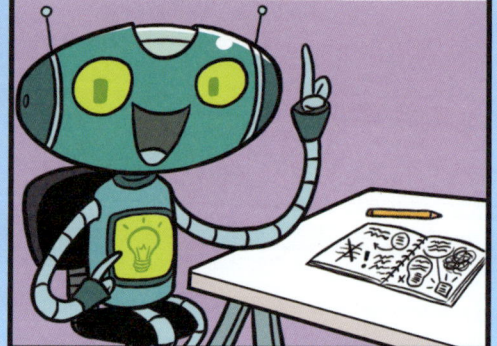

If you know how, you can also create comics using a computer or tablet. But you'll still need the last two things on the list!

GETTING STARTED WITH DRAWING

YOU'RE ABOUT TO DO A *LOT* OF DRAWING. HERE'S A GREAT METHOD USED BY MANY COMIC ARTISTS ...

STEP 1: USE A PENCIL TO SKETCH OUT A VERY ROUGH IDEA OF HOW YOU WANT YOUR PICTURE TO LOOK. THESE SKETCHES ARE KNOWN AS 'THUMBNAILS' BECAUSE THEY USED TO BE DRAWN AS SMALL AS A THUMBNAIL. (DO NOT DRAW ON YOUR THUMB.)

This doesn't have to be perfect! You can fix anything you don't like later.

STEP 2: NOW USE YOUR PENCIL TO DRAW OVER YOUR FIRST SKETCH WITH FIRMER LINES. THIS IS A GOOD TIME TO ADD SOME DETAIL OR FIX ANYTHING YOU AREN'T HAPPY WITH.

STEP 3: GREAT! NOW GET YOUR PEN AND DRAW OVER THE FIRM LINES. BE CAREFUL NOT TO SMUDGE THE INK WITH YOUR HAND AS YOU GO. ONCE THE INK IS DRY, USE YOUR ERASER TO RUB OUT THE PENCIL LINES.

USE THIS EMPTY SPACE TO HAVE A PRACTISE.

GETTING TO KNOW
SPEECH BALLOONS

YOU'LL ALREADY RECOGNIZE SPEECH BALLOONS FROM THE EARLIER PAGES OF THIS BOOK, BUT DID YOU KNOW THAT THEY COME IN LOTS OF SHAPES AND SIZES?

This is the most common type of speech balloon, and is used for normal speech. Notice how the pointy tail is coming from me because I'm the one talking.

A spiky balloon like this one means I'm SHOUTING!

A dashed line means I'm whispering. Shh!

And these cloud-shaped balloons show what I'm thinking.

YOU COULD TRY USING DIFFERENT STYLES OF BALLOONS AND WRITING TO SUIT YOUR CHARACTERS. BLEEP! BLOOP!

A scary monster might have a more MONSTROUS balloon. Grrrr!

Remember to write the words first and draw the balloon around them afterwards, or you might run out of space.

NOW IT'S YOUR TURN. WHAT DO YOU THINK THESE CHARACTERS ARE SAYING? GRAB A PEN OR PENCIL AND FILL IN THE BLANKS. REMEMBER, THERE'S NO WRONG ANSWER – THEY CAN BE SAYING WHATEVER YOU WANT!

GETTING TO KNOW
SOUND EFFECTS

SOUND EFFECTS TELL THE READER ABOUT ANY NOISES IN YOUR COMIC. IT'S TIME TO GET **LOUD**!

ALL OF THE WORDS YOU CAN SEE IN THIS SCENE ARE EXAMPLES OF SOUND EFFECTS. NOISY, RIGHT?

BAROOM!

SPLOOOSH!

CRASH!

THE BEARS

FZZZ ZZZ

HONK!

TICK! TOCK!

WAAAH!

PEW!

PEW!

WHOOOSH!

Sorry! Was that too loud?

TRY ADDING YOUR OWN SOUND EFFECTS TO THESE SCENES. YOU COULD USE THE EXAMPLES FROM THE OPPOSITE PAGE OR MAKE UP YOUR OWN.

CREATING AND USING
PANELS

COMICS USE BOXES, KNOWN AS PANELS, TO MOVE THE STORY ALONG, LIKE THIS ...

Hi! I'm a character, just strolling along minding my own business. Isn't it great to be alive?

REMEMBER, READ THE PANELS FROM LEFT TO RIGHT.

Now that is one BIG boulder.

THIS PANEL SHOWS THE SCENE FROM FURTHER OUT, TO REVEAL MORE.

Ugh.

TRY FILLING IN THE THIRD PANEL WITH SOMETHING FROM YOUR OWN IMAGINATION. WHAT DO YOU THINK HAPPENS NEXT?

Behold ... my latest creation!

WHAT DO YOU THINK THEY'RE LOOKING AT?

Gasp!

It's hideous!

PANELS ARE OFTEN RECTANGULAR, BUT THEY DON'T HAVE TO BE. THEY CAN COME IN ALL SORTS OF SHAPES AND SIZES.

THEY CAN BE WOBBLY, LIKE THIS ONE.

OR THEY MIGHT BE EXPLOSION-SHAPED, LIKE THIS ONE.

SOMETIMES THEY HAVE NO BORDER AT ALL, LIKE THIS ONE.

I just had the oddest dream.

BANG!

I've never felt so free!

THE PANELS IN THE COMIC BELOW HAVE SOME SLIGHTLY MORE INTERESTING SHAPES. CAN YOU DRAW WHAT'S HAPPENING IN THEM?

Hmm, an old lamp. I wonder what will happen if I rub it.

CREATING COOLER PANELS

IN WHAT OTHER WAYS CAN YOU USE COMIC PANELS TO TELL YOUR STORY? HERE'S SOME INSPIRATION.

IT'S NOT JUST THE SHAPE OF YOUR PANEL THAT'S IMPORTANT – IT'S THE SIZE. THINK ABOUT WHAT NEEDS TO FIT IN YOUR PANEL BEFORE YOU DRAW IT.

If the panel is too big, your artwork might get lost.

Hellooooooo!

If the panel is too small, your artwork might look squished.

If you vary the size of the panels on the page, it can make your comic look more interesting.

You're it!

No, you are!

I. WANT. MORE. CAKE.

I don't feel well.

When a page is filled by one big panel, it's called a splash page. Here's one I'm working on at the moment. Can you help me finish it?

BOOOM!

WHAT IS OUR HERO LEAPING TOWARDS? MAYBE THERE'S A GIANT TRAMPOLINE OR A ROARING DINOSAUR? IT'S UP TO YOU!

WHAT TO PUT IN YOUR PANELS

USING PANELS IN DIFFERENT WAYS CAN HELP YOU TO TELL YOUR STORY.

Sometimes, it's good to start off with a location shot, like this, so that readers know where your story is set.

A WIDE PANEL LIKE THIS ONE CAN BE GREAT FOR SHOWING LANDSCAPES.

WIDE PANELS ARE ALSO USEFUL WHEN YOU NEED TO SHOW TWO OR MORE CHARACTERS NEXT TO EACH OTHER.

This is an establishing shot. It lets readers know where your characters are in relation to each other.

IF ALL YOU WANT TO DO IS SHOW ONE CHARACTER TALKING, THEN A HEAD AND SHOULDERS SHOT CAN BE ENOUGH.

CLOSE-UPS, LIKE THIS, ARE GREAT FOR SHOWING EMOTION.

EXTREME CLOSE-UPS CAN SHOW REALLY STRONG EMOTIONS.

THE CLOSER YOU GET, THE MORE EXTREME THE EMOTION.

Too close! You're scaring me!

Ouch! That's my eye! Back up a little!

This comic is about three brave knights who go on a quest to find a dragon — but find something else instead. Use what you've learned in the last few pages to complete the tale.

WOAH!

WHAT HAVE THE KNIGHTS DISCOVERED?

WHAT HAPPENS NEXT? REMEMBER TO USE SPEECH BALLOONS AND SOUND EFFECTS IF YOU NEED THEM.

23

NOW THAT YOU KNOW ALL ABOUT PANELS, IT'S TIME TO PRACTISE! DRAW WHAT YOU LIKE IN THESE PANELS AND CREATE SOME PANELS OF YOUR OWN.

REMEMBER, PANELS DON'T ALL HAVE TO BE RECTANGLES WITH STRAIGHT LINES. HAVE FUN WITH THEM!

This comic has some speech balloons and panels, but no art. Can you finish it off for me?

Oh, it's you! So great to see you again!

WHO IS THE SECOND CHARACTER IN THIS PANEL AND WHAT ARE THEY SAYING?

What do you have there?

PERHAPS THIS PANEL COULD SHOW A CLOSE-UP OF THE SECOND CHARACTER'S HANDS HOLDING SOMETHING UNUSUAL.

GASP!

Be careful with that, or ...

CHAPTER 2
GETTING STARTED

CREATING COOL CHARACTERS

COOL COMICS NEED COOL CHARACTERS! BUT HOW DO YOU COME UP WITH YOUR OWN?

There are loads of different types of characters you could put in your comics. Here's just a tiny selection of examples.

GHOST

PIRATE

DETECTIVE

NINJA

ZOMBIE

ELF

ASTRONAUT

SUPERHERO

ALIEN

SCHOOLKID

CAVEMAN

VAMPIRE

WRESTLER

POP STAR

COWGIRL

MONSTER

WANT TO MAKE YOUR CHARACTERS MORE ORIGINAL?
TRY CREATING SOME MASH-UPS, LIKE THIS ...

NINJA + ASTRONAUT = NINJA-NAUT!

HAVE A GO AT DRAWING THIS ONE YOURSELF.

CAVEMAN + ZOMBIE = CAVE-ZOMBIE!

WHAT COULD YOU MASH UP WITH A VAMPIRE? DRAW IT IN HERE!

VAMPIRE + _____ = _____

Think about what people might expect to see from your character, and flip it around. For example, you might have a knight who is scared of everyone. Or a fluffy kitten that's really ferocious!

GETTING TO KNOW YOUR CHARACTER

IT'S TIME TO GET TO KNOW YOUR LEAD CHARACTER. THE BETTER YOU KNOW THEM, THE EASIER IT'LL BE TO CREATE STORIES ABOUT THEM.

THINK ABOUT WHAT YOUR CHARACTER WANTS MORE THAN ANYTHING ELSE IN THE WORLD. IS IT ...

MONEY?	FAME?	PEACE AND QUIET?	LOVE?

NOW THINK ABOUT WHAT YOUR CHARACTER CAN DO BETTER THAN ANYONE ELSE. DO THEY HAVE ANY SPECIAL SKILLS, SUCH AS ...

FLYING?	STRENGTH?	SPEED?	INTELLIGENCE?

You're going to want more than one character in your comic, so why not make copies of this page? Then you can use it over and over again.

USE THE SPACE BELOW TO WRITE DOWN ALL THE MOST IMPORTANT INFO ABOUT YOUR CHARACTER.

NAME: _____

NICKNAME: _____

AGE: _____

HOME: _____

BEST FRIEND: _____

WORST ENEMY: _____

SPECIAL SKILL: _____

CATCHPHRASE: _____

FAMILY: _____

WHAT DO THEY WANT MOST? _____

_____

WHAT ARE THEY MOST AFRAID OF? _____

_____

DRAW YOUR CHARACTER HERE.

HOW YOUR CHARACTERS INTERACT

ADD A SECOND CHARACTER AND YOU'RE WELL ON YOUR WAY TO HAVING A STORY. BUT HOW DO THEY RELATE TO EACH OTHER?

YOU'LL USUALLY WANT YOUR CHARACTERS TO HAVE SOME SORT OF CONNECTION TO EACH OTHER. ARE THEY ...

BEST FRIENDS?

SWORN ENEMIES?

TEACHER AND STUDENT?

WORK COLLEAGUES?

MADLY IN LOVE?

FAMILY?

ONE WAY OF COMING UP WITH AN INTERESTING STORY IS TO INTRODUCE YOUR LEAD CHARACTER TO SOMEONE WHO IS THE OPPOSITE OF THEM.

My name is X-Com and I'm the opposite of Com-X. I HATE comics!

IN COMICS, LOTS OF RELATIONSHIPS ARE BASED ON ONE PERSON HAVING MORE POWER THAN THE OTHER. YOU CAN MAKE FUNNY OR INTERESTING STORIES BY REVERSING THAT POWER. FILL IN THE EMPTY SPEECH BALLOONS IN THESE TWO COMICS TO FLIP THE POWER!

I'm the teacher! You have to do what I say!

I'm the King! You have to do what I say!

THE COMICS ON THESE TWO PAGES ALL SHOW CHARACTERS INTERACTING WITH EACH OTHER IN DIFFERENT WAYS, BUT THEY'RE INCOMPLETE. CAN YOU FINISH THEM OFF?

Detective Hardcase, let me introduce you to your new partner ...

A monkey, eh?

Take this sword. It's magical and very important.

Why are you giving this to me now?

WHAT DO YOU THINK THE DETECTIVE AND THE MONKEY WOULD BE SAYING TO EACH OTHER?

WHAT WOULD THE WIZARD SAY? DRAW WHAT HAPPENS NEXT.

Doctor Squid! Your reign of evil stops now!

There's something I think you should know ...

What?

EMOTIONAL

HOW WILL YOUR STORY MAKE
YOUR CHARACTERS FEEL ...
AND HOW DO YOU SHOW IT?

HERE ARE SOME EMOTIONS YOUR CHARACTERS COULD
BE FEELING, AND SIMPLE WAYS OF SHOWING THEM ...

HAPPY	SAD	SCARED	SURPRISED	IN LOVE

SMUG	DEVIOUS	DISGUSTED	SHY	LAUGHING

EVIL	GRUMPY	CONFUSED	TIRED	ANGRY

TAKE YOUR CHARACTERS ON AN EMOTIONAL JOURNEY! HAVE A PRACTISE BY DRAWING EMOTIONS ON TO THESE FACES. SOME ARE ON THE OPPOSITE PAGE, BUT SOME YOU'LL HAVE TO THINK ABOUT.

HAPPY ➡ SAD

DISGUSTED ➡ LAUGHING

SHY ➡ BRAVE

BORED ➡ EXCITED

GRUMPY ➡ DISAPPROVING

CONTENT ➡ AWKWARD

IF YOU HAVE CHARACTERS WHO AREN'T HUMAN, THEY MIGHT HAVE DIFFERENT WAYS OF SHOWING HOW THEY FEEL.

I can show my emotions on my screen!

HOW DO YOU THINK THESE CHARACTERS FEEL IN THESE SITUATIONS? COMPLETE THE SCENES BY DRAWING IN THE CHARACTERS' EMOTIONS.

NOW HAVE A GO AT FINISHING OFF THESE TWO THREE-PANEL COMICS. TRY TO SHOW THE CHARACTERS' EMOTIONS EACH TIME.

Almost there ...

What? Kittens?!

WOULD THE SAFE-CRACKER FEEL ANNOYED ABOUT THERE BEING NO MONEY IN THE SAFE, OR HAPPY ABOUT FINDING ALL THOSE KITTENS?

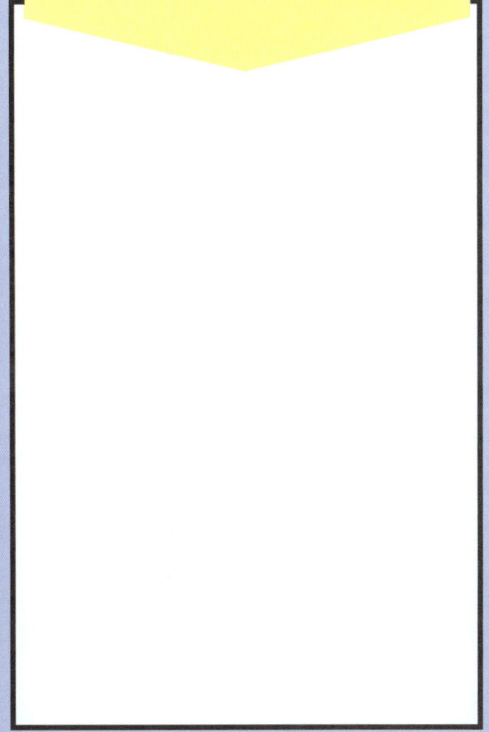

Wow! You got me a present!

WHAT'S IN THE BOX? IS IT GOOD OR BAD? DRAW WHAT HAPPENS NEXT.

HOW HAS THE PRESENT MADE COM-X FEEL? DRAW IT HERE.

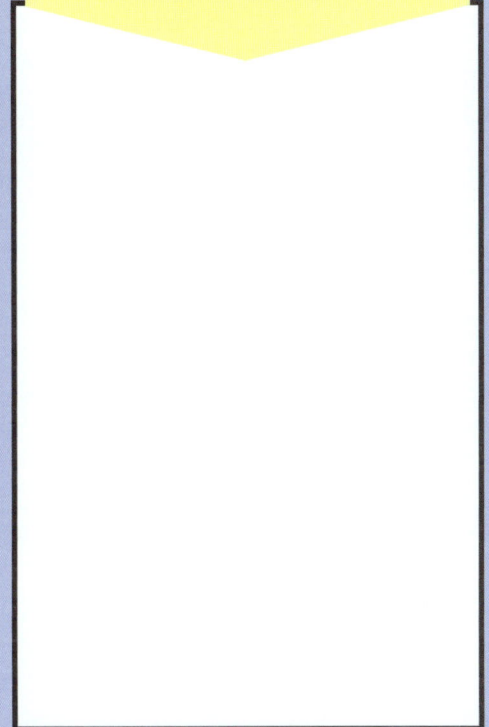

DRAWING
PEOPLE

WANT SOME REALISTICALLY SHAPED PEOPLE IN YOUR COMICS? HERE ARE SOME TIPS FOR DRAWING THEM.

START OFF BY DRAWING A HEAD. MAKE SURE YOU LEAVE SPACE FOR THE REST OF THE BODY. A HUMAN IS NORMALLY ABOUT EIGHT HEADS HIGH.

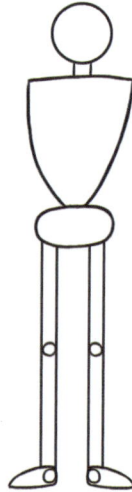

THE TORSO IS ABOUT TWO-AND-A-HALF HEADS HIGH, AND THE LEGS ARE ABOUT FOUR HEADS HIGH.

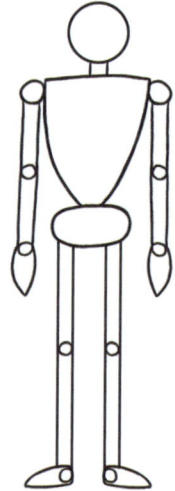

NOW ADD THE ARMS. THEY COME DOWN LOWER THAN THE WAIST.

NEXT, JOIN EVERYTHING UP AND ADD SOME MORE DETAILS.

NOW IT'S YOUR TURN. DRAW A PERSON OF YOUR OWN!

Why can't you all be robots like me? Humans are so much harder to draw!

OF COURSE, YOUR CHARACTERS DON'T HAVE TO LOOK REALISTIC. HERE ARE SOME HUMAN CHARACTERS, SOME WITH VERY EXAGGERATED PROPORTIONS. HAVE A GO AT COPYING THEM, THEN SEE IF YOU CAN DRAW YOUR OWN.

USE THIS SPACE TO PRACTISE DRAWING YOUR OWN HUMAN CHARACTERS. DON'T WORRY ABOUT TRYING TO MAKE THEM LOOK REALISTIC IF YOU DON'T WANT TO. HAVE FUN WITH THEM!

BODY LANGUAGE

EMOTIONS DON'T JUST SHOW ON THE FACE. A CHARACTER'S BODY CAN SAY A LOT ABOUT HOW THEY'RE FEELING.

CHECK OUT HOW THIS SAME SIMPLE FIGURE CAN SHOW ALL SORTS OF FEELINGS WITH JUST A FEW ADJUSTMENTS ...

EXCITED	BORED	SICK	ANGRY

PLAYFUL	TIRED	CONFIDENT	SURPRISED

HERE ARE SOME CHARACTERS YOU MIGHT LIKE TO INCLUDE IN YOUR COMICS. CAN YOU RE-DRAW EACH ONE TO SHOW HOW THEY'RE FEELING?

DRAW THIS ADVENTURER ... EXCITED.

DRAW THIS SPACE EMPEROR ... SCARED.

DRAW THIS GOBLIN ... UNHAPPY.

NOW YOU KNOW HOW TO CREATE CHARACTERS, GET THEM INTERACTING WITH EACH OTHER AND SHOW HOW THEY FEEL. USE THE NEXT FEW PAGES TO BRING ALL THESE THINGS TOGETHER IN SOME COMIC IDEAS OF YOUR OWN.

Remember what you learned about panels in chapter one, and finish off this page and the next one with some of your own.

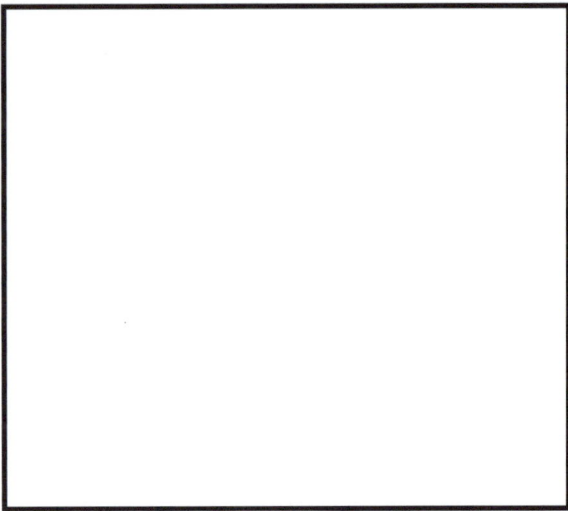

Still not sure about how to turn all of this into a cool story that really works? The next chapter should help!

CHAPTER 3
TELLING YOUR STORY

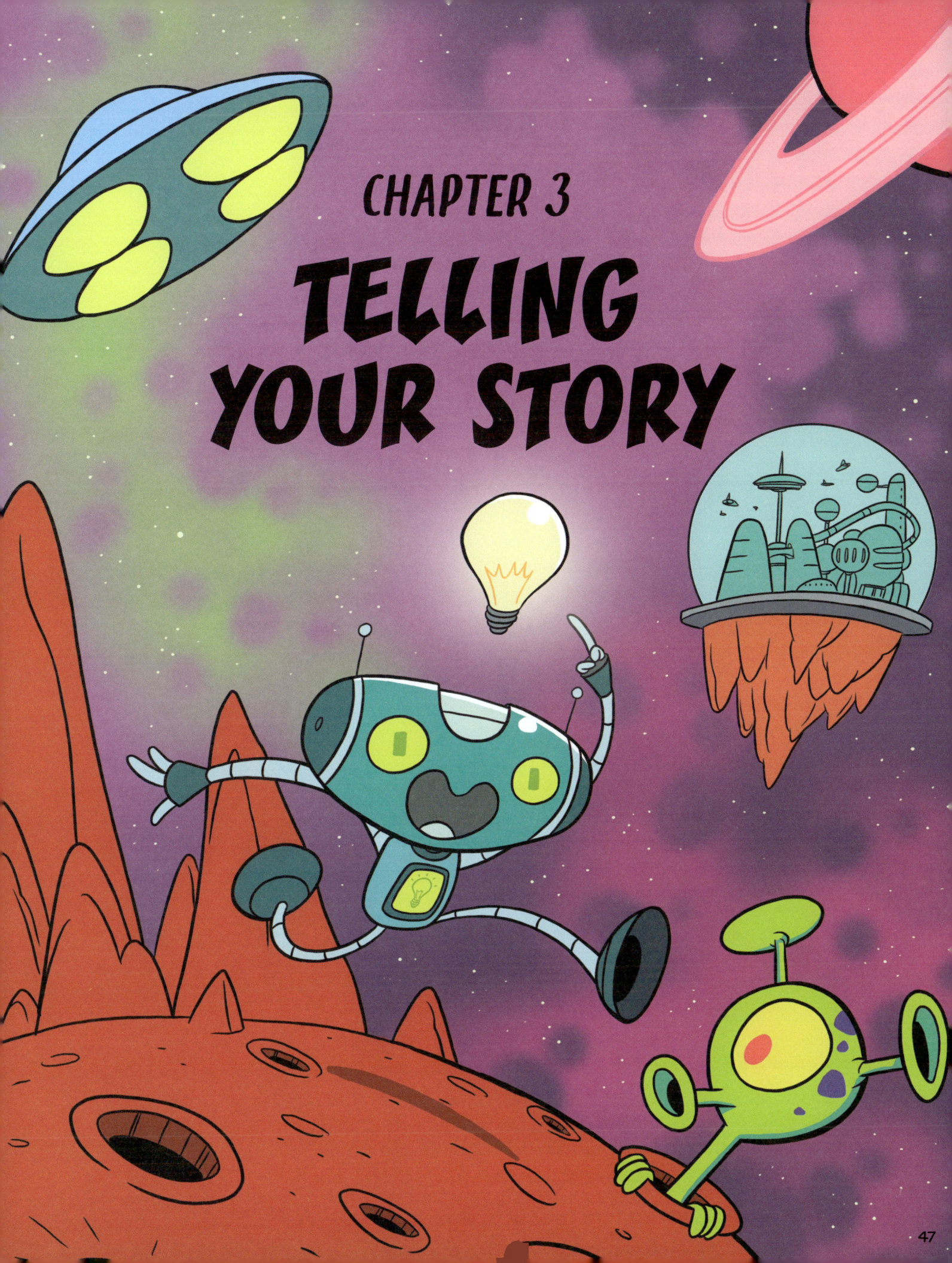

FINDING YOUR
STYLE

WHAT TYPE OF ART WILL YOU USE TO TELL YOUR STORY?

THERE ARE LOADS OF DIFFERENT COMIC ART STYLES OUT THERE. HOW DO YOU LIKE TO DRAW?

IF YOU DRAW IN A CARTOONY STYLE, READERS WILL PROBABLY EXPECT YOUR STORY TO BE FUNNY.

IF YOUR CHARACTERS LOOK MORE LIKE SUPERHEROES, PEOPLE MIGHT EXPECT AN ACTION STORY.

BLACK-AND-WHITE ART CAN BE GREAT FOR SERIOUS STORIES, SUCH AS THE ONES YOU FIND IN DETECTIVE COMICS.

MORE REALISTIC ARTWORK CAN SUGGEST THAT YOUR COMIC IS ABOUT REAL LIFE.

FINDING YOUR STYLE CAN BE TRICKY. HERE'S AN EXERCISE THAT MIGHT HELP YOU FIND THE STYLE THAT WORKS BEST FOR YOU.

FLIP BACK TO PAGE 28 OF THIS BOOK AND CHOOSE ONE OF THE CHARACTERS AT RANDOM. NOW DRAW THAT CHARACTER IN THREE DIFFERENT WAYS, IN THE SPACE BELOW. YOU DON'T HAVE TO COPY THE WAY THEY'RE DRAWN IN THIS BOOK. YOU COULD DO A REALLY SIMPLE VERSION, A REALLY DETAILED VERSION OR A COMPLETELY WACKY VERSION WITH HUGE EYES OR SUPER-LONG LEGS. HAVE FUN AND DO YOUR OWN THING!

WHICH STYLE ARE YOU HAPPIEST WITH? TRY USING THAT STYLE IN THE NEXT COMIC YOU DRAW.

Remember, there's no wrong style. Go with the style you enjoy drawing and feel happiest with!

INTRODUCING COMIC
GENRES

JUST LIKE MOVIES AND TV SHOWS, COMICS FALL INTO CATEGORIES CALLED GENRES. WHICH GENRE APPEALS MOST TO YOU?

PEOPLE EXPECT DIFFERENT THINGS FROM DIFFERENT GENRES. FOR EXAMPLE ...

SCIENCE FICTION

READERS EXPECT:
• SPACE TRAVEL
• ALIENS
• COOL GADGETS AND TECH

SUPERHERO

READERS EXPECT:
• SUPERPOWERS
• SECRET IDENTITIES
• BATTLES BETWEEN GOODIES AND BADDIES

DETECTIVE

READERS EXPECT:
• A MYSTERY TO SOLVE
• LOTS OF SUSPECTS
• A COMPLICATED CRIME

FANTASY

READERS EXPECT:
• BIG, EPIC STORIES
• MAGIC, WIZARDS AND DRAGONS
• NO MODERN TECHNOLOGY

HORROR

READERS EXPECT:
• SCARY GHOSTS OR MONSTERS
• PEOPLE IN DANGER
• HAUNTED HOUSES AND GRAVEYARDS

COMEDY

READERS EXPECT:
• JOKES
• SILLY CHARACTERS
• FUNNY SITUATIONS

A GREAT WAY OF STARTING OFF YOUR STORY IDEAS
IS TO COMBINE DIFFERENT GENRES, LIKE THIS ...

HORROR   **+**   COMEDY   **=**   HORROR-COMEDY

NOW YOU TRY! FILL IN THE EMPTY SPACES BELOW WITH YOUR OWN GENRE
MASH-UPS. YOU CAN PICK GENRES FROM THE PREVIOUS PAGE OR GO FOR
SOMETHING ELSE ENTIRELY. ADD YOUR OWN DOODLES FOR THE GENRES, TOO.

_____   **+**   _____   **=**   _____

_____   **+**   _____   **=**   _____

Just because people expect
something from a genre
doesn't mean you have to
do it. Pack your comic
with surprises!

WHAT HAPPENS NEXT?

EACH OF THESE COMICS FITS INTO A DIFFERENT GENRE. CAN YOU FINISH THEM OFF?

COMEDY

DOES THE CHICKEN HAVE A FUNNY ANSWER FOR COM-X?

Why are you crossing that road?

FANTASY

WHAT DOES THE WIZARD'S MAGIC DO TO THE DRAGON?

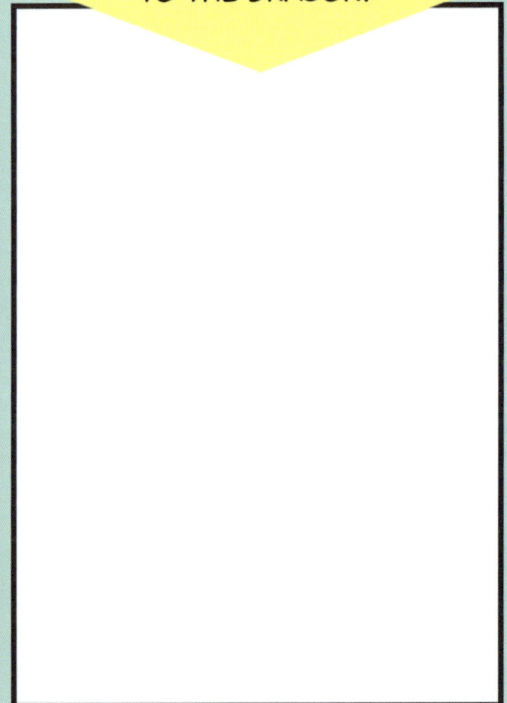

RAAAH! This dragon is invincible!

We'll see about that!

That's the last of those alien ships!

PEW! PEW!

BOOM!

And now to do what I came here to do ...

WHAT DOES THE PILOT DO NEXT?

HORROR

Welcome ... TO MY HOUSE OF HORROR!

DO THE KIDS VENTURE INSIDE THE VAMPIRE'S HOUSE? IF THEY DO, WHAT TERRORS AWAIT THEM INSIDE?

53

CHOOSING YOUR
LOCATION

THE SETTING YOU GIVE YOUR COMIC CAN BE JUST AS IMPORTANT AS THE CHARACTERS YOU PUT IN IT.

HERE ARE SOME FUN PLACES WHERE YOUR STORY COULD START ... OR FINISH.

A CASTLE

A JUNGLE

AN ALIEN PLANET

AN ANCIENT TEMPLE

A PIRATE SHIP

A HAUNTED HOUSE

A FUTURISTIC CITY

SOMEWHERE YOU JUST THOUGHT OF (DRAW THIS ONE YOURSELF)

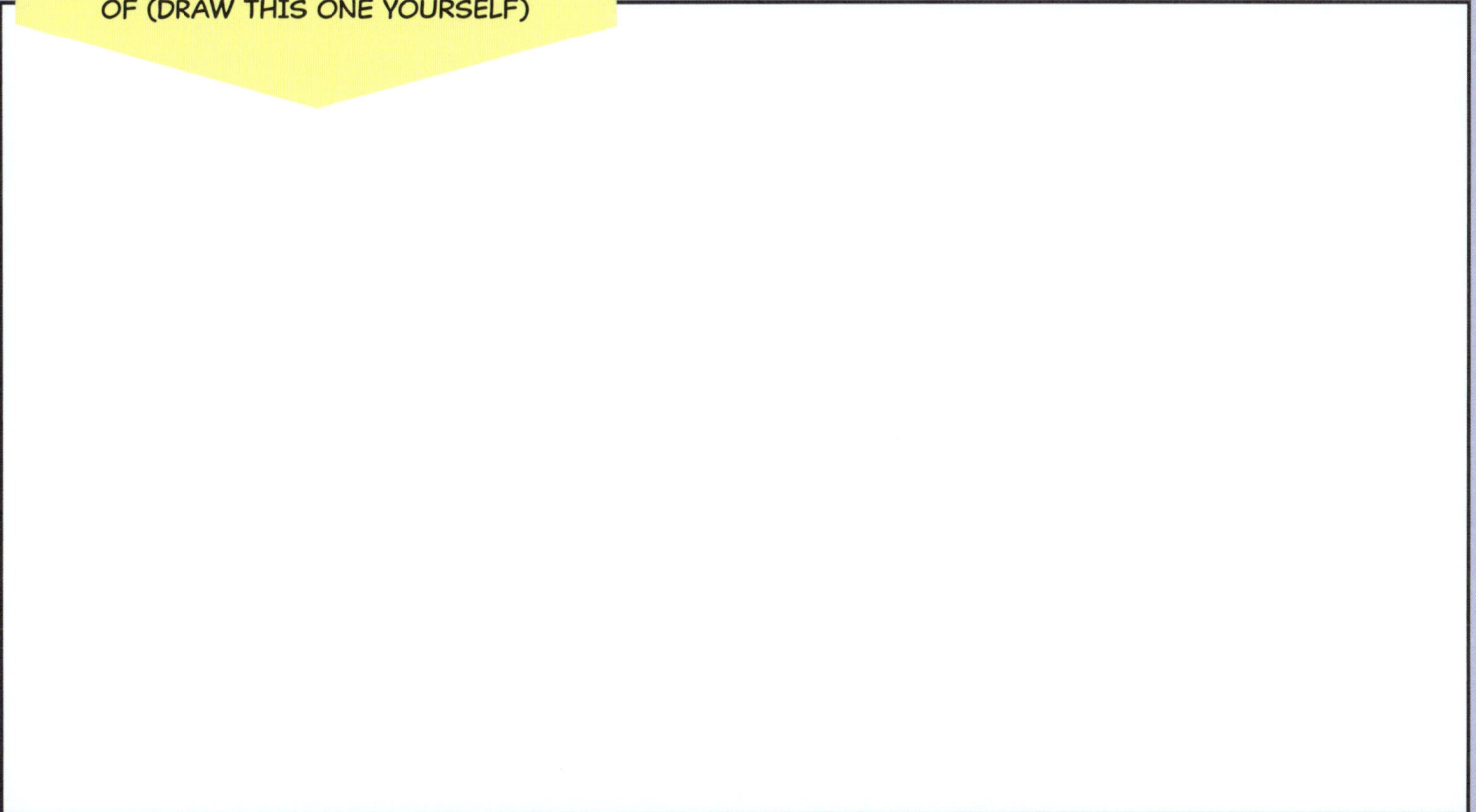

WHERE ARE

THEY?

THESE PANELS ALL HAVE CHARACTERS, BUT NO LOCATION. USE YOUR OWN IMAGINATION TO DRAW THEIR LOCATIONS AROUND THEM.

WHERE MIGHT YOU FIND A GOBLIN AND AN OGRE DOING BATTLE?

BRINGING IT ALL TOGETHER

NOW YOU KNOW ALL ABOUT CHARACTERS, GENRES AND LOCATIONS – BUT HOW DO THEY ALL FIT TOGETHER?

SOME THINGS ARE OFTEN FOUND TOGETHER IN STORIES. FOR EXAMPLE ...

A VAMPIRE IN A HORROR STORY IN A CREEPY CASTLE

AN ASTRONAUT IN A SCI-FI ADVENTURE ON AN ALIEN PLANET

Your characters can be in any place, time or location you like. It's your story, after all!

THESE THINGS DON'T SEEM TO BELONG TOGETHER AT ALL – BUT WHAT IF YOU PUT THEM TOGETHER ANYWAY?

+ +

A PRINCE IN A COMEDY AT A ROCK CONCERT

+ +

A DINOSAUR IN A DETECTIVE STORY UNDER THE SEA

NOW GIVE IT A GO YOURSELF!

+ +

A _____ IN A _____ IN A _____ ? GENIUS!

REMEMBER THAT WEIRD MIX OF CHARACTER, GENRE AND LOCATION YOU CAME UP WITH AT THE BOTTOM OF THE PREVIOUS PAGE? IT'S TIME TO FIND OUT IF IT WORKS! USE EVERYTHING YOU'VE LEARNED SO FAR (AND THESE PANELS) TO TURN IT INTO A TWO-PAGE COMIC OF YOUR OWN.

A BIG, WIDE PANEL LIKE THIS ONE WOULD BE AN IDEAL PLACE TO DRAW YOUR LOCATION.

THESE SMALLER PANELS COULD BE GOOD PLACES TO SHOW YOUR READER SOME CLOSE-UPS.

REMEMBER, PANELS DON'T ALWAYS HAVE TO BE BOXES. COULD YOU USE THIS SPACE TO TRY SOMETHING DIFFERENT?

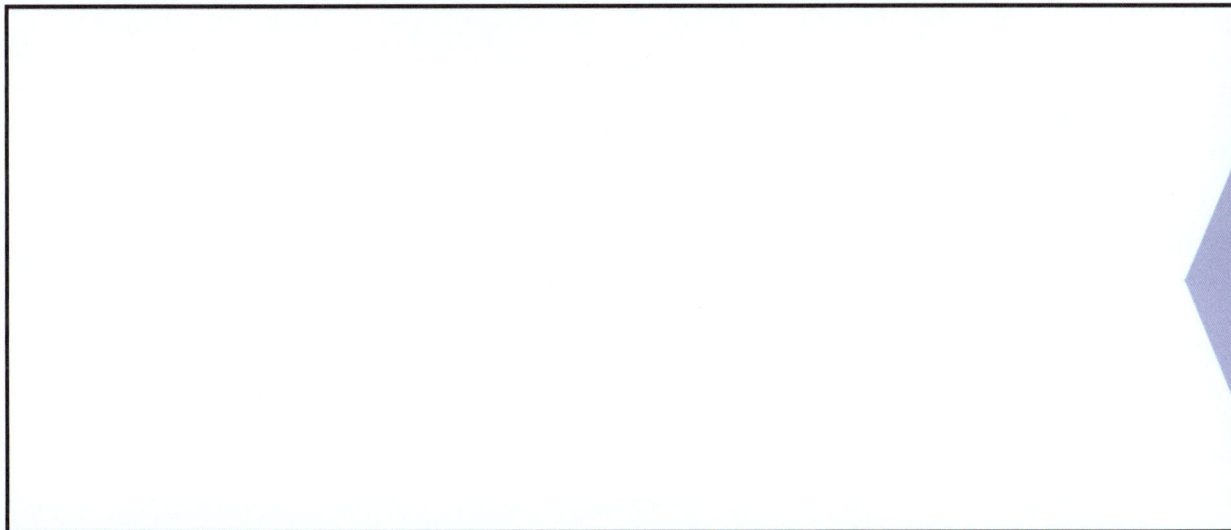

STRUGGLING WITH YOUR ENDING? THE REST OF THIS CHAPTER SHOULD HELP.

PLOTTING YOUR COMIC:
THE BEGINNING

EVERY STORY NEEDS A BEGINNING, A MIDDLE AND AN END. HERE ARE SOME FUN WAYS TO START YOURS.

THE BEGINNING OF YOUR STORY LETS THE READER KNOW WHAT TO EXPECT AND TELLS THEM A BIT ABOUT THE MAIN CHARACTER.

I love to read comics!

EEK!

YOU COULD START BY DRAWING YOUR CHARACTER AT HOME. IT'S A GOOD WAY OF SHOWING WHO THEY ARE AND WHAT THEY LIKE TO DO.

I'm Com-X! Nice to meet you.

Hmph!

COMIC

INTRODUCING YOUR CHARACTER TO SOMEONE NEW RIGHT AT THE START IS A GOOD WAY OF INTRODUCING THAT NEW PERSON TO THE READER, TOO.

YOU COULD EVEN START YOUR COMIC IN THE MIDDLE OF THE ACTION. IT'S A GREAT WAY TO GRAB YOUR READER'S ATTENTION.

THESE THREE-PANEL COMICS EACH HAVE AN END, BUT NO BEGINNING.
FILL IN THE BLANK PANELS TO START THEM OFF.

PLOTTING YOUR COMIC:
THE MIDDLE

THE MIDDLE OF YOUR STORY IS OFTEN THE MOST FUN PART. IT'S THE REASON YOU STARTED TELLING THE STORY IN THE FIRST PLACE.

YOU'VE INTRODUCED THE READER TO YOUR CHARACTERS. WHAT ARE THEY GOING TO DO NEXT?

THEY COULD GO ON A JOURNEY TO SOMEWHERE THEY'VE NEVER BEEN BEFORE ...

... OR THEY MIGHT DECIDE TO TRY SOMETHING NEW ...

... OR PERHAPS THEY NEED TO STOP SOMEONE ELSE FROM DOING SOMETHING.

I'm going to destroy all the comics in the world! Mwa-ha-ha!

Stop!

COMIC

IN THE MIDDLE OF THE STORY, YOUR CHARACTER WILL USUALLY HAVE TO FACE DIFFERENT CHALLENGES. HERE ARE SOME DIFFERENT KINDS OF CHALLENGES THEY MIGHT COME UP AGAINST.

MENTAL CHALLENGES

CHALLENGES OF STRENGTH

CHALLENGES OF WILLPOWER

PHYSICAL CHALLENGES

Your character doesn't have to succeed first time at everything they do. Sometimes, if we see someone trying hard and failing, it makes us care about them more.

PLOTTING YOUR COMIC:
THE END

THE ENDING IS THE MOST IMPORTANT PART OF ANY STORY. HOW WILL YOUR CHARACTERS END UP?

HERE ARE SOME COMMON TYPES OF ENDING ...

HAPPY ENDING: THE MAIN CHARACTER GETS WHAT THEY WANT. HOORAY!

UNHAPPY ENDING: THE VILLAIN GETS WHAT THEY WANT. BOO!

UNCLEAR ENDING: THE READER HAS TO MAKE UP THEIR OWN MIND ABOUT WHAT HAPPENED.

Com-X ... I am your father!

NOOO!

PLOT-TWIST ENDING: EVERYTHING WE THOUGHT WE KNEW WAS WRONG.

CLIFFHANGER ENDING: THE STORY ISN'T FINISHED AT ALL! LET'S HOPE THERE'S A SEQUEL.

HOW DO YOU THINK THIS COMIC SHOULD END? IT'S UP TO YOU.

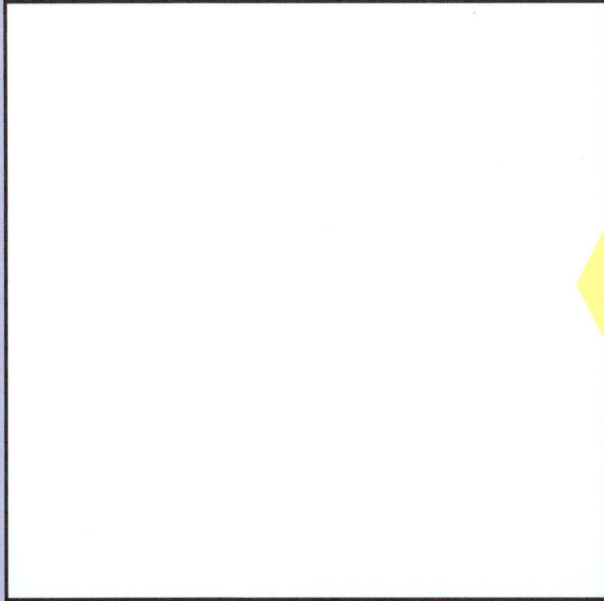

I think I have an idea ...

DOES OUR HERO MANAGE TO DEFEAT THE ALIENS? OR DOES SOMETHING UNEXPECTED HAPPEN?

Once you have your ending, go back and make sure the rest of the story still works. You might decide to make some changes to the beginning or middle.

BEGINNING

MIDDLE

END

THE SEARCH FOR A
STORY

EACH OF THESE CHARACTERS NEEDS JUST ONE THING: A STORY! CAN YOU COME UP WITH AN IDEA FOR EACH ONE? THE FIRST ONE HAS BEEN DONE FOR YOU.

NAME: Captain Cowardly

THEIR STORY: A nervous superhero who is scared of everything is forced to overcome their own fears when the rest of the world's superheroes are kidnapped.

NAME: _____

THEIR STORY: _____

_____

_____

_____

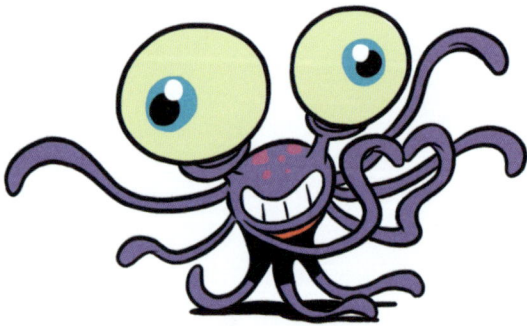

NAME: _____

THEIR STORY: _____

_____

_____

_____

NAME: _____

THEIR STORY: _____

_____

_____

_____

NAME: _____

THEIR STORY: _____

_____

_____

_____

NAME: _____

THEIR STORY: _____

_____

_____

_____

NAME: _____

THEIR STORY: _____

_____

_____

_____

NAME: _____

THEIR STORY: _____

_____

_____

_____

WHAT'S YOUR PLOT?

IT'S TIME TO PLAN A WHOLE STORY OF YOUR OWN. USE THESE PAGES TO WRITE, DRAW AND SCRIBBLE DOWN YOUR IDEAS.

ONCE UPON A TIME THERE WAS A ...

USE THIS SPACE TO DRAW SOME ROUGH SKETCHES OF YOUR CHARACTERS.

WHO WAS FRIENDS WITH ...

THEY LIVED IN ...

THEY LOVED TO ...

If you're struggling, try not to overthink it. What happens if you just write down the first idea that pops into your head? Give it a go!

SO, EVERY DAY, THEY ...

ONE DAY, SOMETHING AMAZING HAPPENED ...

BECAUSE OF THIS AMAZING THING, SOMETHING ELSE HAPPENED ...

THEY LOVED TO ...

TURN THE PAGE TO CONTINUE PLANNING YOUR STORY.

BUT THEN ...

AND SO ...

WHICH MEANT THAT ...

UNTIL FINALLY ...

CHAPTER 4
YOUR COMICS

MAKE SOME BRILLIANT
COMICS

THERE'S ONLY ONE THING LEFT TO DO – AND THAT'S MAKE LOADS OF COMICS OF YOUR VERY OWN!

THIS FINAL CHAPTER OF THE BOOK IS FULL OF IDEAS TO HELP YOU KICK-START YOUR IMAGINATION. ON THE NEXT FEW PAGES, YOU'LL FIND A WHOLE BUNCH OF NEW COMICS TO GET CRACKING WITH.

It's time to use everything you've learned so far and let your imagination run wild! The only rule is ... THERE ARE NO RULES!

Each of the comics in this chapter is only a page long, but you don't have to stop there. If you want your story to be longer, grab another piece of paper and keep it going.

If you'd like more inspiration, help is at hand! Head to pages 86 to 91 to try out the Story Generator tools.

The goal is wide open! I can do this ...

Wait ... what's going on?

You'll never stop me!

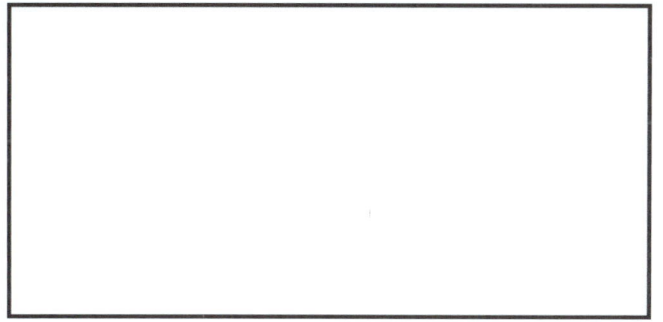

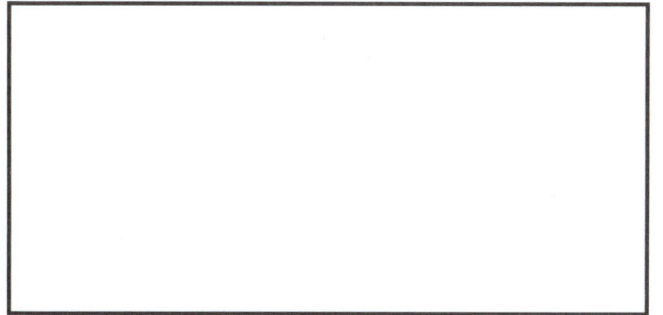

PIRATES! COMING STRAIGHT FOR US!

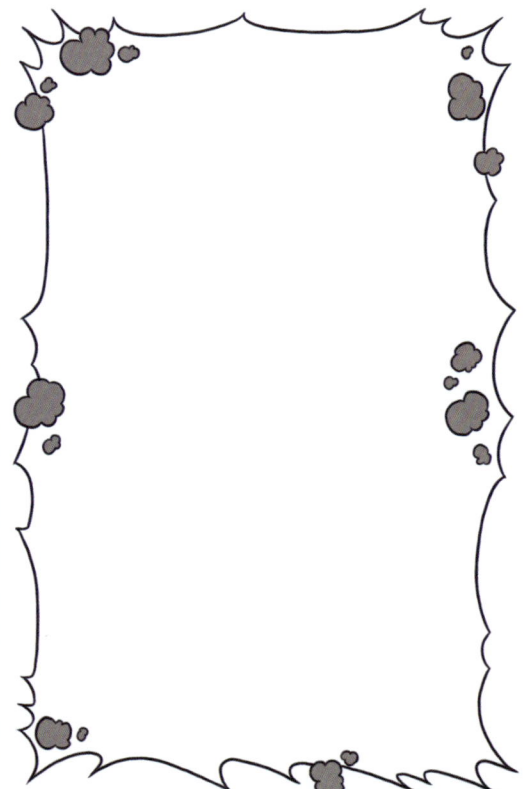

STORY GENERATORS

EVEN THE VERY BEST COMIC WRITERS AND ARTISTS FEEL STUCK FOR IDEAS SOMETIMES. ON THE NEXT FEW PAGES, YOU'LL FIND A FEW DIFFERENT TOOLS FOR KICK-STARTING YOUR IMAGINATION. TRY THEM OUT AND SEE HOW YOU GET ON!

STORY GENERATOR 1

FOR THIS ONE, ALL YOU NEED IS A DICE. ROLL IT AND LET THE NUMBERS DECIDE WHERE YOUR STORY TAKES YOU.

FIRST, FIND OUT YOUR GENRE ...

1. COMEDY
2. HORROR
3. DETECTIVE
4. SCIENCE FICTION
5. SUPERHERO
6. FANTASY

NOW HEAD TO YOUR GENRE AND ROLL THE DICE AGAIN TO FIND OUT WHAT YOUR STORY IS GOING TO BE ABOUT ...

COMEDY

1. A SCHOOL FOR PRACTICAL JOKERS
2. TWO BEST FRIENDS WHO GET INTO TROUBLE
3. A FUNNY ANIMAL WHO KEEPS GETTING THINGS WRONG
4. A STRONG HERO WHO IS VERY STUPID
5. A SCIENTIST WHO COMES UP WITH A SILLY INVENTION
6. A KID WHO IS ALWAYS DAYDREAMING

HORROR

1. A SCHOOL FOR MONSTERS
2. A WEREWOLF WHO BECOMES A CELEBRITY
3. A HAUNTED SWEET SHOP
4. A GHOST DOG
5. A CLUMSY MUMMY
6. A FAMILY OF VAMPIRES

DETECTIVE

1. A SCHOOL FOR SPIES
2. A DETECTIVE WHO IS SECRETLY ALSO A CRIMINAL
3. A CRIMINAL WHO IS SECRETLY ALSO A DETECTIVE
4. A PLAN TO STEAL SOME PRICELESS JEWELS
5. A CRIME-SOLVING CAT
6. A CRIME IN SPACE

SCIENCE FICTION

1. A SCHOOL FOR ALIENS
2. A TIME MACHINE THAT GOES WRONG
3. TOO MANY CLONES!
4. AN EPIC BATTLE IN SPACE
5. A ROBOT THAT MIGHT BE EVIL
6. A SPACESHIP THAT GETS LOST

SUPERHERO

1. A SCHOOL FOR SUPERHEROES
2. A SUPERHERO WHO IS SECRETLY A VILLAIN
3. A TEAM OF SUPERHEROES WHO CAN'T STOP ARGUING
4. A KID WHO WANTS TO BE A SUPERHERO
5. A SUPERHERO WITH A TERRIBLE SECRET
6. A SUPERHERO WHO LOSES THEIR POWERS

FANTASY

1. A SCHOOL FOR WARRIORS
2. A QUEST FOR A MAGIC SWORD
3. A FIRE-BREATHING DRAGON WHO JUST WANTS A FRIEND
4. THE WORLD'S WORST WIZARD
5. GOBLINS ATTACK EVERYONE!
6. A MAGIC MIRROR THAT CAN SEE THE FUTURE

Remember, these are just starting points to get your brain whirring. If you land on something and want to change it, then go for it!

STORY GENERATOR 2

THIS TIME, TRY USING YOUR PERSONAL INFO TO CREATE A STORY IDEA.

1. USE THE FIRST LETTER OF YOUR FIRST NAME.

MY STORY IS ABOUT A ...

A ASTRONAUT
B KNIGHT
C GORILLA
D CELEBRITY
E ELF
F SPY
G SCHOOLKID
H THIEF
I VAMPIRE
J DRAGON
K ROBOT
L CAT
M WEREWOLF
N UNICORN
O VIKING
P PIRATE
Q PRINCE OR PRINCESS
R ALIEN
S MONSTER
T SKELETON
U DOG
V EXPLORER
W HAWK
X GHOST
Y SUPERHERO
Z MONKEY

2. USE THE FIRST LETTER OF YOUR SECOND NAME.

WHO IS ALSO A ...

A ARTIST
B SCIENTIST
C TIME-TRAVELLER
D WARRIOR
E PARENT
F DOCTOR
G CHEF
H WITCH OR WIZARD
I NINJA
J GAMER
K GIANT
L DANCER
M IMAGINARY FRIEND
N FARMER
O INVENTOR
P VILLAIN
Q LIFEGUARD
R POLICE OFFICER
S GAME-SHOW HOST
T TEACHER
U DINOSAUR EXPERT
V PILOT
W VET
X PLUMBER
Y MERMAID OR MERMAN
Z FOOTBALLER

Try using the names and birthdays of your family and friends to get different stories!

3. USE THE MONTH OF YOUR BIRTHDAY.

THEY HAVE TO ...

JANUARY	GO ON A JOURNEY
FEBRUARY	FIND A HIDDEN TREASURE
MARCH	HIDE FROM DANGER
APRIL	SAVE A LOT OF PEOPLE
MAY	SOLVE A CRIME
JUNE	WIN A RACE
JULY	DEFEAT AN ENEMY
AUGUST	DISCOVER SOMETHING
SEPTEMBER	TRIUMPH IN A BATTLE
OCTOBER	BECOME FAMOUS
NOVEMBER	LEARN AN IMPORTANT LESSON
DECEMBER	MAKE A NEW FRIEND

4. USE THE DAY OF YOUR BIRTHDAY.

BUT THERE'S AN OBSTACLE ...

1. THEY'RE SCARED OF CHANGE
2. THEY DON'T KNOW HOW TO DO WHAT THEY NEED TO DO
3. THEY'RE MANY MILES AWAY FROM WHERE THEY NEED TO BE
4. THEY DON'T HAVE ANY MONEY
5. THEY HAVE BEEN CURSED
6. THEIR FAMILY DOES NOT APPROVE
7. A PLAGUE IS TURNING PEOPLE INTO ZOMBIES
8. THE GOVERNMENT HAS MADE WHAT THEY NEED TO DO ILLEGAL
9. A MYSTERIOUS PROPHECY TELLS THEM THEY WILL FAIL
10. THEY HAVE BEEN MAGICALLY TRANSFORMED INTO A MYTHICAL CREATURE
11. A MASSIVE VOLCANO ERUPTS
12. THEY'VE PROMISED SOMEONE THEY WON'T DO THE THING THEY NEED TO DO
13. THERE ARE SCARY CREATURES THAT COME OUT EVERY NIGHT
14. THEY SWAP BODIES WITH SOMEONE ELSE
15. THEY'RE ACCUSED OF A CRIME THEY DIDN'T COMMIT
16. THEY BECOME STRANDED ON A DESERT ISLAND
17. A METEORITE IS ABOUT TO HIT THE EARTH
18. A CHILDHOOD RIVAL IS TRYING TO STOP THEM
19. A GREEDY BILLIONAIRE STANDS IN THEIR WAY
20. THEY ARE HANDED A GREAT RESPONSIBILITY
21. THERE'S A HUGE FLOOD
22. A MONSTER IS RAMPAGING THROUGH THEIR HOME
23. THEIR HOME PLANET GETS INVADED
24. THEY HAVE A SUPERPOWER, BUT THEN THEY LOSE IT
25. A SUPERVILLAIN ATTACKS
26. A MYSTERIOUS ORGANIZATION WANTS TO STOP THEM
27. THEIR HOUSE FALLS DOWN
28. THEY HAVE TO OVERCOME A FEAR
29. THEY LOSE THEIR MEMORY
30. THEY GO TO SLEEP FOR 100 YEARS
31. THEY'RE SHRUNK TO THE SIZE OF A TADPOLE

STORY GENERATOR 3

FEELING READY TO CREATE A MORE COMPLEX STORY? ASK A FRIEND TO RANDOMLY PICK NUMBERS FROM EACH OF THESE LISTS, AND SEE WHAT YOU GET.

GENRE MASH-UP! ASK YOUR FRIEND TO PICK TWO NUMBERS FROM THIS LIST AND COMBINE THE GENRES TOGETHER.

1. DRAMA
2. HORROR
3. DETECTIVE
4. THRILLER
5. COMEDY
6. SCIENCE FICTION
7. WESTERN
8. FANTASY
9. SUPERHERO
10. FAIRY TALE

AT LEAST PART OF YOUR STORY SHOULD TAKE PLACE IN ...

1. AN OCEAN
2. A HAUNTED HOUSE
3. A SAILING SHIP
4. A DISTANT PLANET
5. A SCHOOL
6. A FUTURISTIC CITY
7. PREHISTORIC EARTH
8. A GOBLIN'S CASTLE
9. A DRAGON'S LAIR
10. A SKYSCRAPER

YOUR STORY MUST INCLUDE AT LEAST ONE ...

1. TALKING ANIMAL
2. DINOSAUR
3. PIRATE
4. GHOST
5. KING OR QUEEN
6. ROBBER
7. CAVEMAN OR CAVEWOMAN
8. ROBOT
9. ARMY GENERAL
10. MOUSE

YOUR HERO HAS ...

1. MAGICAL POWERS
2. A SUPER-FAST MODE OF TRANSPORT
3. FAME AND FANS
4. GREAT INTELLIGENCE
5. A HIDDEN IDENTITY
6. A FUNNY SIDEKICK
7. SUPERHUMAN STRENGTH
8. A COLOURFUL COSTUME
9. A CLOSELY KEPT SECRET
10. A FEAR TO OVERCOME

YOUR VILLAIN HAS ...

1. AN UNDERGROUND BASE
2. THEIR OWN ARMY
3. AN EVIL LAUGH
4. A BUNGLING HENCHMAN OR HENCHWOMAN
5. LOTS OF MONEY
6. AN ARMOURED VEHICLE
7. A VERY SHORT TEMPER
8. A PLAN TO TAKE OVER THE WORLD
9. A GRUDGE AGAINST YOUR HERO
10. A SCARY MASK

UP FOR AN EXTRA CHALLENGE? CHUCK ONE OF THESE INTO YOUR STORY, TOO!

1. A MYSTERIOUS GLOWING ORB
2. A SAFE FULL OF STOLEN TREASURE
3. A HIGH-SPEED CHASE
4. A DREAM
5. AN INCREDIBLE DISCOVERY
6. A CHICKEN
7. A KNOCK ON THE DOOR
8. A TEDDY BEAR
9. A CREATURE WITH VERY SHARP TEETH
10. A BIG PARTY

NOTES AND IDEAS

GLOSSARY

THE COMIC WORLD HAS LOTS OF ITS OWN TERMS AND PHRASES THAT CAN SOMETIMES BE TRICKY TO REMEMBER. HERE ARE SOME OF THE MAIN ONES USED IN THIS BOOK, AND WHAT THEY MEAN.

BALLOON
THE BUBBLE THAT APPEARS NEXT TO CHARACTERS AND CONTAINS THEIR SPEECH. BALLOONS ARE OFTEN ROUND, BUT CAN COME IN LOTS OF OTHER SHAPES, TOO.

COMIC
A SEQUENCE OF PICTURES THAT ARE USED TO TELL A STORY. COMICS CAN CONTAIN ONLY A FEW PICTURES OR BE MANY PAGES LONG.

ESTABLISHING SHOT
A PICTURE THAT SETS UP WHERE YOUR CHARACTERS ARE. IT'S OFTEN A LARGE PICTURE, SHOWING YOUR CHARACTERS FROM SOME DISTANCE IN ORDER TO LET THE READER SEE MORE OF THEIR SURROUNDINGS.

GENRE
A CATEGORY OF STORY THAT IS RECOGNIZABLE FROM ITS CHARACTERS, LOCATION OR PLOT. EXAMPLES OF GENRES INCLUDE HORROR, SCIENCE FICTION AND FANTASY. SOMETIMES, DIFFERENT GENRES CAN BE MIXED TOGETHER IN ONE STORY TO CREATE SOMETHING UNEXPECTED OR UNUSUAL.

GRAPHIC NOVEL
A LONG COMIC THAT OFTEN FORMS AN ENTIRE BOOK.

LANDSCAPE
THE SURROUNDING AREA, SUCH AS BUILDINGS, MOUNTAINS OR FIELDS.

LOCATION SHOT
A PICTURE THAT HAS THE PURPOSE OF SHOWING WHERE YOUR STORY IS SET. FOR EXAMPLE, A LOCATION SHOT COULD SHOW THE INSIDE OF A ROOM, THE TOP OF A MOUNTAIN OR A BUSY CITY STREET.

PANEL
THE FRAME THAT IS USED TO CONTAIN THE PICTURES IN A COMIC. A PANEL IS OFTEN JUST A SQUARE OR RECTANGLE, BUT CAN BE ANY SHAPE OR SIZE. PANELS ARE PLACED NEXT TO EACH OTHER IN SEQUENCE SO THAT READERS KNOW WHAT PART OF THE COMIC TO READ NEXT.

SOUND EFFECT
A WORD THAT IS USED TO SHOW THE READER THAT A NOISE CAN BE HEARD.

SPLASH PAGE
A PAGE THAT CONTAINS JUST ONE BIG COMIC PANEL. A SPLASH PAGE COULD BE USED TO SHOW THAT LOTS OF THINGS ARE HAPPENING AT ONCE OR SHOW A SCENE IN GREATER DETAIL, OR JUST TO MAKE A PARTICULARLY EXCITING SCENE AS STRIKING AS POSSIBLE.

TAIL
THE SMALL, POINTY BIT THAT LEADS FROM THE BALLOON TO THE CHARACTER, AND SHOWS THE READER WHO IS SPEAKING.

THUMBNAIL
A VERY ROUGH SKETCH THAT COMIC ARTISTS USE WHEN PLANNING THEIR STORIES. THUMBNAILS CAN BE EASILY RUBBED OUT OR CHANGED, BECAUSE THEY HAVEN'T BEEN COLOURED IN OR FINISHED YET.

ONE LAST COMIC STORY IDEA FROM ...

NED HARTLEY

(THIS BOOK'S AUTHOR)

A YOUNG BOY HAS THE POWER TO TURN INTO A CAT WHENEVER HE LIKES. IN CAT FORM HE CAN GO ALMOST ANYWHERE HE WANTS, BECAUSE HE CAN SQUEEZE THROUGH SMALL SPACES. ONE DAY, HE SNEAKS INTO A VET'S BY MISTAKE AND GETS CAPTURED IN A CAT CARRIER! HOW DOES HE ESCAPE?

ONE LAST COMIC STORY IDEA FROM ...

ALEX LOPEZ

(THIS BOOK'S ILLUSTRATOR)

A PIRATE T. REX AND HER DINOSAUR CREW LAND ON A MYSTERIOUS ISLAND IN SEARCH OF TREASURE. ON THEIR WAY ACROSS THE ISLAND, THEY ARE ATTACKED! WHO ATTACKS THEM AND WHY? AND WHO WINS?